Dana Malcolm

Our brave boys.

A memorial discourse, delivered in the Second Congregational church,

Norwich, Conn., December 10th, 1865

Dana Malcolm

Our brave boys.
A memorial discourse, delivered in the Second Congregational church, Norwich, Conn., December 10th, 1865

ISBN/EAN: 9783337727185

Printed in Europe, USA, Canada, Australia, Japan

Cover: Foto ©ninafisch / pixelio.de

More available books at **www.hansebooks.com**

Our Brave Boys.

A

MEMORIAL DISCOURSE,

DELIVERED IN THE

SECOND CONGREGATIONAL CHURCH,
NORWICH, CONN.,

DECEMBER 10TH, 1865,

BY M. M. G. DANA,

PASTOR OF THE CHURCH.

PUBLISHED BY REQUEST.

NORWICH:
BULLETIN JOB PRINTING OFFICE,
1866.

"Dulce et decorum est pro patria mori."

MEMORIAL.

JOHN IV. : 38.

OTHER MEN LABORED, AND YE ARE ENTERED INTO THEIR LABORS.

It has ever been a beautiful sentiment which has prompted mankind to honor their worthy and illustrious dead. And so it has been customary in almost every age to celebrate their virtues and deeds in poems and eulogies, by monuments of granite, and statues of marble. The world can not afford to do without the memory of its benefactors. Whatever is noble and self-sacrificing deserves to be perpetuated. By the ordering of Providence, it is intended that the honored and useful should pass into history; for sepulture was never synonymous with oblivion.

So invested is every human life with relations that give it significance and influence, that the words of sacred writ have special force;—" For none of us

liveth to himself, and no man dieth to himself."
Children mourn for parents. Communities lament
the death of leading citizens. The demise of a Prince
carries sorrow through an empire, or the sudden de-
cease of a President drapes a Republic in sorrow,
while for the fallen heroes, upon whose swords hung
the destinies of nations the people grieve, and bear
them in sadness to their burial.

We never tire in our grateful tribute to our ances-
tors,—who sought on this continent a new home,
who endured the hardships incident to its settle-
ment, and then cheerfully gave their lives to
transmit it to us free. Ready are our praises for
their successors, who augmented what they inheri-
ted, and bequeathed in turn to us with well guarded
institutions of liberty and learning, the States they
dwelt in and the Government they maintained. And
it is in keeping with this just practice of the past,
that we render our homage to those who have more
recently sacrificed their ease and their lives to preserve all that we to-day possess. Through all these
instances we observe the principle enunciated in
the text,—other men labored; we have entered
into their labors. Others bear the burdens; we

enjoy the results. They fought and fell; we live secure and prosperous.—It is the method by which all our benefits are procured. Every privilege costs some one a struggle. It is the solemn law of vicarious sacrifice; a law which pervades all nature, and penetrates even the realm of human existence. It is the deep mystery of all being,—the sacrificing of life to give life.

The decaying rock forms the soil in which the herb grows up. The corn of wheat dies, and out of this death comes the harvest-life. The layers of deciduous leaves shelter the tree-roots, and form the rich substance in which the young shrubs start to vigorous growth. So, too, in the animal world, the hawk strikes down the dove; the smaller fishes are food for the larger; myriad forms of higher life sustain themselves by preying on the weaker and more helpless; and in like manner it is impossible for man to live, as it is for man to be redeemed, except through vicarious suffering. Every human being has its birth in this law of sacrifice. No blessing comes to man save through this law. Every country cleared for civilization and made attractive for human abodes, cost the first settlers the hardships and

early death incident to pioneer life. For its inde-
pendence of foreign rule, and a free government of
its own, patriots must battle and die. For its preser-
vation when assailed by traitorous hands, must the
loyal-hearted contend. So that there never was a
victory won, but those who took possession of the
conquest passed over the bodies of the noblest slain.
It is this which invests with sanctity every social
and religious right,—for they were all the price of
blood. The Christian Church, with its precious hopes
and holy inspirations, was procured by the Blood of
Christ, and has been perpetuated through the ages by
the sacrifices of its martyrs and confessors. Civil freedom has grown fastest when its roots were moist-
ened by the blood of those who died in its behalf.
Truth itself has all the while advanced by planting
its feet in the blood of friends, and anon in that of
foes, swinging, like a mighty pendulum, from one
joy to another disaster, while the hands on the dial-
plate above show how steadily it has moved on.

And when we remember all that was imperiled
by the late rebellion, we shall anew appreciate the
patriotism of those who stood for our defence. A
high-hearted, puissant nationality, with its array

of arts and industries, of laws and institutions, saved
to us and our posterity ;—assuredly, if this be the result of others' sacrifices, it exalts their worth and
entitles them to our lasting gratitude.

But when it is borne in mind that more than this
was the consequence of their service, who will un-
dertake to measure the debt we owe those fallen
heroes. Our Nation—redeemed from the thralldom
of injustice, shaking off the badges of its history's
shame, appearing in its new power, like "the
clear shining after rain,"—is the monument to
their great labors. The Republic anew committed to
the Justice and Liberty which its founders had valued, made aware of the supremacy of principles over
forces, is their memorial. And because of their
achievements, its history to us will be nobler and
more full of inspiration, while a share in their labors will all people claim. The progress of Liberty
throughout the world has by them been made more
rapid, and the foretokenings of the millenial day
to be more certainly discerned. They have re-
established our Liberties and our Government, and
their exhilarating example abides to stir us to generous emulation. Colossal evils, which had grown

with our growth and threatened our national life
have been overthrown, and new principles are in
the ascendant. The banner of the nation waves once
more over an undivided land, its unchallenged sove-
reignty supreme from the Lakes to the Gulf. Institutions which were the fairest bloom of the ages and
the brightest promise of the race, their heroic courage and sacrifice have preserved intact. All this is
the result of their having labored and died, and this
is the grand legacy they have left us to enjoy.

We can win no more laurels in a war for self-
defence; other hands have gathered them. To us
remains the duty of mastering the civil problems
yet unsolved, and of fashioning the institutions
which are to mould the spirit of the nation. Their
labors have illustrated the capacity of Christianized
men to maintain a democratic government,—to hold
a country in the interests of freedom, where the feet
of slaves shall scorch no more the soil, nor the breath
of traitors poison the air. They have vindicated
before the world that a great nation has no right to
die, and that unresisted assassination is virtual sui-
cide. Through their prowess the unfulfilled promises of the Fathers have been realized.

As in times of peace we are not apt to weigh the sacrifices that it costs to procure our blessings, let our yet close proximity to these days of war and woe, serve to exalt our estimate of the noble spirits that stood in the place of mortal peril to preserve and perpetuate them. By the side of the patriots of the Revolution, these latest defenders of the country take their place. We cherish every memorial of such illustrious heroes,—we admire their patience and fortitude; for every day of peace, with its new development of greatness to the land and glory to its institutions, proclaims the magnitude of those labors upon which we have entered. The story of their sufferings and successes shall take significance from the era of the nation's new birth and power.

As Americans and as Christians we pay this slight tribute to the memory of our noble dead, and record our gratitude for what through them has given to life new joys and promise. As we gather the rich fruitage of the tree of Freedom planted by our fathers and defended by their children, we here will not cease to remember those who went from our homes,—from this Church and Sabbath School. Forever precious shall be the names of these our own
2

martyr heroes, who delivered us from peril, and made our peace more sacred and secure. Honored boys, who in the freshness of their opening manhood were counted worthy to suffer and die,—their memory is embalmed in our hearts and their example inspires us to better life. While yet the dew of youth was on them, they cheerfully exposed their lives for our menaced rights, and by the casualty of battle have fallen martyrs to Liberty and Law. Henceforth none need be uncertain how far the loyal sentiment reaches and how much it carries with it. Our Constitution and Laws will be more sacred than we ever thought them to be; our very name and heritage more august.

It is with the purpose of recalling their noble patriotism, and of commending their example to those who knew them well, that this Memorial has been prepared. It is a record that the Sabbath School with which these brave boys were all at some time connected, may well prize. I remember what an impression the simple reading of their names produced on me, as I first saw them inscribed on the Sabbath School walls, and encircled with evergreen. *" Our brave boys,"* was the simple but touching in-

scription over the names I have come personally to
cherish with deepest reverence. Learning, moreover,
that they were all Christian young men, I thought
they were eloquent preachers of piety as well as
patriotism to their surviving comrades.

It seemed fitting, therefore, that now as the war
has closed, and the principles for which they fought
and fell are triumphant, some final tribute of gratitude should be paid to their memories; and that we
should seek to perpetuate, for the sake of the School
and Church where they received religious instruction,
the record of all they did and endured. One look
upon the land their young valor defended, noting
the happiness with which it is filled and the fame it
has acquired abroad, will assure us that even the
smallest testimonial to those whose sacrifices procured all this, is not out of place. Many of
those who hazarded their lives in the same great
cause, have by a merciful Providence been permitted to return. They, with us, enjoy the fruit of their
own labors and the labors of their comrades in
arms. But those whose manly forms are missed
from our assembly to-day, whose voices we no
more shall hear in prayer and praise,—they who

died, not having seen the end or enjoyed the victory, we commemorate by this imperfect tribute of our grateful love.

And while indulging in the recollections which cluster about these lives we watched and saw so early cease, let us remember that we have duties and obligations corresponding to the blessings purchased for us. Allowed to partake of the fruit of their patriotic toils, may we seek jealously to preserve and extend the principles for which they fought. Blessing God that they lived and labored, the remembrance of what they accomplished shall inspire in us a new courage concerning the future, and stimulate us to loftier achievement. Prompt to honor and commemorate our dead, may we by our labors serve as much the country and its liberties for which they became willing sacrifices. A brief sketch of each of those who went from our school, and who never returned, will serve to awaken a new appreciation of their character and career.

Sergeant JAMES TORRANCE was the youngest son of a widowed mother, born Nov. 29th, 1841, near Edinburgh, Scotland. He possessed in a high degree the qualities of self-reliance and integrity which characterize so generally the Scotch. With a bright earnest face, a manly form, those who observed him in the Sabbath School class, or in the workshop, were attracted by his appearance. While there was nothing in it particularly striking, there was still a quiet earnest bearing which impressed you. At the first call of the Government for troops, he promptly responded, and went out with the Third Connecticut Regiment, commanded by Col. Terry, and was in the Battle of Bull Run. Returning with the regiment, he was not contented to remain at home. His heart was in the cause, and he longed once more to enroll himself among the country's defenders. Though his mother sought to retain him by her side, reminding him that she was now dependent upon her boys, he still seemed to think it was her duty to give him up, and his to go. Balancing thus the claims of a beloved mother, for whom he cherished the reverent affection peculiar to those of his nation, and the claims of his adopted country, he was for some time in much perplexity as to the course to be pursued.

Meanwhile, his mother noticed the boy's strong

desire to enlist once more, and was not wholly unprepared for the decision which brought him again to that step. "Mother," he said, as nearly as his words can now be recalled, "you know we have adopted this as our land, and we ought in this hour of peril to do something for the Government, and I think I ought to enter its service." The time had come, and sorrowfully, yet hopefully, the fond parent replied, "Jamie, if you must go, one condition I have to propose,—that you will read a chapter in this Testament, (handing him the copy,) when not on duty, every night at nine o'clock, and your mother will do the same; and so we will remember each other." He assented to this, and in the Thirteenth Regiment, under the gallant Colonel, now Major General Birge, he soon took his departure for the Department of the South, under the command of Gen. Butler. The record of the regiment in New Orleans, where it was the body-guard of the commanding general, and its subsequent career in the Port Hudson campaign, attest its high character. Young Torrance was regarded in his company as a brave and upright soldier, and his captain reports him as one of the most reliable in his command.

Sabbath, April 27th, 1862, he united with the
Regimental Church, partaking for the first time of
the Lord's Supper. It was in fulfilling the promise
made to his mother, that he was thus brought to
the Saviour. Throughout his journal, I find the
frequent entry,—" Read my chapter this evening,"
and sometimes the statement, " omitted my chapter
to-night in consequence of duty," or something else
which necessarily prevented him. Conscientiously
adhering to what was right, he was one of the few
men, says his captain, who kept his moral character
unblemished. From his journal, I noted the scru-
pulousness with which he attended divine service :
and in one place he makes the entry, " took the
guard to a temperance meeting to-night." In many
ways this regard for his own and others' moral and
religious welfare, is revealed. Patient and perse-
vering, he kept up his hope in the final triumph of
the Government over its domestic foes.

His letters home abound in pleasant descriptions
of all that he saw and experienced, and contain
the evidence of an unaltered devotion to those from
whom he was parted. After his religious change, he
wrote more solemnly of the exposure of his life, and

---

assured his mother " that now he was prepared for death." Intelligently comprehending all the issues of the war, he as a Christian thought also of his own personal peril. And it seemed a relief to him, as it was a source of great joy to his anxious mother, that he had given his heart to Christ, and that now whatsoever might befall him, it would still be well with him. So his loyalty led him towards religion; the two fires burning together, one helped kindle the other. Assuredly there is a relation too deep for all to see between true loyalty and piety. Devotion to one's country, with its history, its laws, its honors of the past, and its promises of a greater future, is kindred to the devotion martyrs have shown, when they sacrificed all for their faith.

In the battles of Georgia Landing, Oct. 27, 1862, and of Irish Bend, April 14, 1863, the regiment saw hard service, and acquired a reputation for courage, steadiness and discipline, unsurpassed by any in the Department. In both these actions Sergeant Torrance acquitted himself with honor. Not afraid to die, he was fearless in the duties of his position, and well seconded by his own example and achievements the orders of his superior officers. On Sabbath, May 24, 1863, was the assault on Port Hudson, with the Thirteenth Regiment in the advance, leading the charge. Just previous to the battle, Torrance remarked to a comrade: "The only thing I dislike in the service, is the being obliged to fight on the Lord's Day, at least commencing any engagement which could as well be postponed till after the passage of holy time." His early training, together with the high national respect paid by his own race to the Sabbath, had brought him to regard it as strictly sacred time. Still, he had of course no option, and he took his position on the line of battle. The conflict was severe and protracted, and though unsuccessful, it was not owing to lack of bravery on the part of the men.

It was in this action that young Torrance received his death shot. After little more than a year's service, he fell, as the hero should fall, facing the foe and leading in the charge. He had staked all in his country's behalf, and died in her defence. His was a humble career, for it was a modest yet manly youth who lived it, who sought ambitiously for no personal renown, but who was earnestly intent on the Government's deliverance. It was the career of a

3

brave Christian boy, who with intelligent patriotism
and unobtrusive fidelity took his place in the ranks,
counting not his own life dear if only the country
might be saved. And just such noble unosten-
tatious boys gave to our armies their constancy
in a long and bloody struggle, and their final victory
over a determined and vindictive foe. I confess
to no slight admiration of those who so conscientiously and quietly labored and suffered for so
glorious a cause. These inconspicuous heroes, un-
heralded by the bulletins of generals, unknown as
they stood in serried column, were our real deliver-
ers; and I honor every one who with a heart to
feel, and a mind to understand the character of the
conflict, fell fighting in the ranks. On the grave of
every such private in an army of heroes, I would
willingly place the cypress tribute, for such sacrifice and valor secured the home and freedom so precious to-day.

His seat in the Sabbath School class is vacant, but
his memory will be fondly cherished, for he honored
us by his manly piety as well as his patriotic devotion. His humble home surrendered a precious of-
fering to secure the greater "home of the free."

His brother, Colonel of the Twenty-ninth Colored Regiment, who has so nobly distinguished himself in this contest, wrote to the mourning mother when he heard the sad intelligence that her son and his brother had fallen :—" Our starry flag where'er it floats will be dearer now to me, hallowed and consecrated by a brother's blood. Let us give thanks that God has accepted our sacrifice, and that we are permitted to do and to suffer in the cause of *Liberty, Right, and Truth.*"

Lieutenant ALFRED M. GODDARD was born in Marietta, Ohio, June 19, 1836. His parents removed to Norwich when he was quite young, and here he grew up, developing a character of rare beauty and force. Leaving his home at an early age to commence life for himself, he for that reason was less generally known than otherwise he would have been. Yet in the home where a peerless devotion to those he most deeply loved distinguished him, by friends who were aware of his noble nature, he was held in reverent and affectionate esteem. None knew him but to admire his earnestness of spirit, his commanding self-reliance, his determined energy; and all this tempered by a refinement and gentleness, which gave to his character unusual completeness.

He was one of those choice spirits whose career is invested with all that can stimulate and instruct. Immersed, when quite young, in the cares and duties of a responsible business, he yet displayed a culture ordinarily looked for only in the man of letters. His criticisms on books that chanced to pass under his notice, betray a fine taste united with unusual analytic power. His journal while in the Pacific, abounds in the most graphic portrayal of life on ship-board, and on the Islands. Susceptible to all that was beautiful and grand in nature, his descriptions of scenery in the Tropics and of the changeful ocean, near and upon which so much of his life was spent, can hardly be surpassed.

Entering, when still under age, the employ of Williams & Haven, of New London, Conn., he was by them sent out to the Sandwich Islands, and in connection with a Branch House, resided about five years at Honolulu. During that period he made several voyages to the Arctic Ocean, passing two years on McKean's Island, in the Southern Pacific. At the breaking out of the war, he was about leaving Honolulu for Mauritius. When the news reached him that hostilities had actually commenced, he was eager to leave at once for home, that he might enroll himself among those hurrying to the Government's defence; but such were his business engagements, that fidelity to his employers required the prosecution of the voyage. So, with a disappointed heart, he endeavored to do the work to which he was committed, though his thoughts were with the brave men who were already marshalled for deadly conflict with our foes.

He writes in his journal as he started on this voyage: " I have been reading the Atlantic Monthly. It is all war. How is this? I am trying to do my duty, and yet a deathly sickness comes o'er me when I think what a feeling of joy it would have given me could I have gone home and given up all for my country." At a later date he adds: " All my hope now is, that having chosen this path I may command myself and give my thoughts to the present, trusting that through some great good luck I may yet find myself among the New England heroes." Who of us imagined that on the far Pacific main there was a heart beating with such lofty pat-

riotism; reckoning as its chiefest trial that it could
not share in our struggle for national existence.
And yet, like thronging doves to their windows
came the patriots of our land, traveling homeward
from every quarter of the globe that they might
swell the hosts who battled for truth and freedom.

He speaks at this time of the change in his views
of life,—" It is so real, so earnest, and can be so noble." Then reverting to his country, he remarks,
" I begin to think the war is the best thing which
could have happened to us. I know it must stir up
our young men to action and fill their veins with
new life. I honor the brave fellows and am proud of
dear old Connecticut. The spirit of our Puritan
Fathers is not yet dead."

While at Mauritius, hearing of his father's sudden
death, young Goddard hastened back with the ut-
most expedition that he might visit his bereaved
mother and mingle with the afflicted family. Taking
the East Indian route through the Red Sea and Europe, he arrived at his home in the fall of 1862. He
hoped then to enter the army and gratify thus the
deepest longing of his heart. But his business engagements compelled him to go back once more to

the Sandwich Islands, and with great reluctance he turned his face toward the Pacific. He seemed at this time keenly sensitive lest his absence from the country while in so critical a condition should not be understood. Many are the journal entries which betray this fear. "If my choice could be recalled," he writes in one place, "I would go through anything to get upon the battle field." As indicative of his religious state while so full of the war-spirit, he says of his last Sabbath at Honolulu: "Spent a pleasant hour at the Young Men's Prayer Meeting, an hour I hope never to forget, nor the promises which my heart made while in communion with those dear friends in Jesus." He speaks also of the moral issues of the conflict, demonstrating his ardent love of liberty for all classes—"It seems strange the country should have been ruled so long by this small party. (Slaveholders.) But the time for a change has come, and I think the curse of slavery will now be removed from our beautiful land."

Despatching with promptness his business at the Islands, and closing his connection with the firm he had served so long and well, he was enabled to return home in May, 1863. Then the cherished purpose of his soul seemed at length possible to be carried out.

On the following July, he received a commission as First Lieutenant in Company B of the Eighth Connecticut Regiment, but was at once detached for duty on the Staff of General Harland, the former Colonel of the Eighth Regiment. In this capacity he rendered faithful service until March, 1864, when, at the request of officers and men, he rejoined his regiment. "It is a hard thing to do," says his diary, "but I am sure it is right." His associates on the Staff parted with him, not without the greatest reluctance and the most genuine regret. To General Harland he was strongly attached, and by him in turn was esteemed as an able officer and a personal friend. The heart which had chafed so when business prevented his connection with the army, was still dissatisfied with the less arduous duties of staff officer, so he took his place in the ranks, and the long yearning of his heart seemed about to be appeased when the hardships and dangers of the field were to be his.

March 13, 1864, the regiment, under command of Col. J. E. Ward, left its old camp at Portsmouth,

Va., and marched to Deep Creek, where it performed outpost and picket duty until April 13. Thence it was ordered to Yorktown, and was assigned to the Second Brigade of the Eighteenth Corps. Forming part of Gen. Butler's command, it was engaged in a reconnoisance of the enemy's lines before Petersburgh. On the morning of May 8, the regiment led the advance in an attempt to press back the enemy. Forming in battle line, it repeatedly charged the foe, driving him before them, and continued fighting till the ammunition was exhausted and the regiment was relieved by order, receiving, as it returned from the bloody field, the cheers of the whole brigade. It was in this action that the fatal bullet struck Lieut. Goddard. While bravely fighting and cheering on his men in this his first battle, he fell, mortally wounded.

The day before, his entry in his diary, when it was apparent an engagement was imminent, was both touching and significant,—" And the Children of Israel prevailed because they trusted in the Lord God of their Fathers." The day of the battle, Saturday, May 7, he wrote:—" 7 A. M. we go to the front with only arms and ammunition." Before sun-

4

down he was borne from the field, and ere another day had gone, the knightly youth of high hopes and unflinching courage passed away. Of his carriage on the day of battle, his captain writes:—"He was so thoughtful and considerate, not rash or impetuous but cool and collected, ready for any emergency, willing for every duty." He had won in no common degree the esteem of officers and men, and his loss was felt by all.

Upon the examination of his wound, he asked the regimental Surgeon whether it was likely to prove fatal, adding, at once, that he thought it must, in which opinion the surgeon was obliged to concur. Immediately he added: "Tell my mother that I die in the front, that I die happy. I have been a great sinner, but Jesus loves me, and I can trust him." Removed to the Chesapeake Hospital, at Fortress Monroe, he lingered for little more than a day, suffering intensely but patiently.

When the Chaplain asked him what he should read, he replied: "Read that hymn 'Just as I am, without one plea.'" All around him were affected by his heroic endurance, and his perfect trust in Christ. To one beautiful thought he gave utterance, (wrote the

regimental Chaplain,) when told he must die—" Then
I shall be free from temptation." And soon *he was;*
sinking into his peaceful rest, as the lengthening
shadows indicated the waning day. Sweet rest he
soon found, after a short life full of adventure and
of noble toil.

Writes one who knew him well : " He was one of
the few men whom I have known in my life whose
steadfast honesty was proof against all temptations,
and his varied life exposed him to not a few." Another friend, intimately associated with him while
in the army, wrote when news of his death was received : " How kind and unselfish he was. What a
sturdy champion for every thing just, noble, and
right. How he loathed oppression and injustice.
How he loved his country."

Few excelled him in the earnestness and unselfish
devotion which so eminently characterized him. A
whole hearted consecration to others' good, made
his career beautiful and his death glorious. In his
grand young strength God permitted him to die,
and his death adds another to the list of heroes
whose memory and example are the Nation's heritage.

Adjutant E. BENJAMIN CULVER was the only son of Benjamin and Adelaide Culver, born in the city of New York, Oct. 27, 1840.

Through his school and business life he became well known here, and by those most intimately acquainted with him, he was esteemed as a young man of more than ordinary excellence and promise. One of his early instructors speaks of him as the "*peace-maker*," while his teacher in Norwich, with whom he spent nearly a year and a half, mentions his marked *truthfulness* of character.

In the Sabbath School no face was more thoughtful, no heart more responsive to the appeals of the truth. By the superintendent he was regarded as one of those stable, upright boys, whom the Sabbath School not only benefits, but whose very presence gives character and success to the school. Earnest in all his views of life, it was a pleasure and a privilege to teach him in reference to the things of heaven. while the same qualities made him a prized member of the little band first engaged in the Mt. Pleasant Mission School. His personal appearance gave all the impression of youthful manliness. Generous in his feelings and self-possessed in his manners, young Culver was the favorite of a large circle of friends. In the spring of 1859, after a season of unusual religious interest, he united with this Church, and maintained thenceforth a high character as a faithful and devoted Christian. His religious experience seemed to give new breadth and beauty to his life. Unassuming, and withal modest in his ways, his was a quiet, but earnest piety. He said little in public about it, yet his daily life witnessed to its power.

His pastor says of this change in his character:—
" In passing from death unto life, he did not profess to experience any rapturous emotions of joy, any strong assurance of hope, but a placid, serene and humble consciousness of a new and living purpose of consecration to the service of the Saviour, and consequent delight in that service." His mother writes, that " he was always thoughtful, and in early years was the subject of deep religious convictions. When but eleven years of age, so impressed was he by a sermon on missions, that he resolved to become a missionary, whenever old enough. This purpose he relinquished, only when failing health indicated that he could not probably endure the labor

incident to such a life. From this time, however, he became a careful student of the Bible, and it was these impressions which culminated in his public profession of Christ in 1859.

As a clerk in the store of Lee & Osgood, he has left the reputation of rare fidelity and skill. Energetic and quick to learn, he mastered the business, and gave promise of great success. Between himself and employers a warm attachment existed, broken only by his early death. His admirable business qualities, as well as his personal worth, had attained for him a position not often reached by those as young as he.

When the Eighteenth Regiment was forming, the duty of entering his country's service came to him with new force. Seeking the advice of friends and parents, he finally registered his conviction of what was duty, by enlisting. The purest of motives prompted him in this act, for it was when his earthly prospects were brightest that he entered the army, and his parents knew that at pecuniary sacrifice he remained in the service. He was moreover an only son, tenderly beloved, and relinquished more than many in leaving father and mother at his country's call.

In August, 1862, he left Norwich with the Eighteenth Regiment, commanded by Col. William G. Ely. While stationed at Baltimore, Culver was detailed to act as clerk at the head-quarters of Gen. Schenck, Commandant of the *Middle Department.* His executive ability secured him the appointment, and so valuable were his services considered by the General, that he was retained some time after his promotion to the Adjutancy of the regiment. While in this position, in one of his letters he speaks of his dissatisfaction with such labor. Though it was safer and more lucrative than a soldier's service, still, he said it was not for this kind of work he enlisted. He was eager to engage in active campaigning—to meet the hardships and brave the perils of the field.

He rejoined his regiment just after the unfortunate battle of Winchester, June 13, 14, 15, 1863, when the Colonel and a large proportion of the officers and men were taken prisoners. His first letter, dated at Maryland Heights, spoke of "a disconsolate band" he had succeeded in gathering together,—the remnants of the splendid regiment which had left

Norwich less than a year previous. He furnished to anxious friends the first reliable account of the casualties of that action. Entering upon the duties of Adjutant, he proved himself at once a most efficient officer.

In April, 1864, he returned home on a furlough, and many remember with deep interest that last visit. The campaign of the spring was about to open, and the indications were that there would be hard fighting. The earnestness with which Culver spoke of the increased perils showed his full appreciation of his own exposure, when he returned. Coming events appeared to have wrought an unusual thoughtfulness. And though he spoke calmly and with hope, it was with a half betrayed impression that this would prove his last interview with Norwich friends. Side by side in our west gallery he sat with a brother officer, a worshiper as of old in this place of prayer. It was the last time he heard his Pastor's voice, the last service he was to attend in the Church where he had confessed his faith in Christ, and enrolled himself as a disciple of the Saviour.

At the last interview with his parents, his mother

remarked: " You look care-worn, but I do not ask
you to resign." He replied : " I could not be induced
so to do, for, dear mother, calmly and deliberately I
give my service, and my life if necessary, for my
country. You remember the lines—

‘ " For strangers into life we come,
And dying is but going home." ’

When he returned to his regiment, the army of
the Shenandoah, of which it formed a part, had
started upon its long and tedious campaign. At
New Market, Va., occurred the first engagement
with the rebels. In this the Eighteenth Regiment
participated, losing fifty-six in killed, wounded and
missing. The report of this battle was the last Adjutant Culver lived to make. Retreating to Cedar
Creek, Va., the army rested several days, and was
reorganized under General Hunter, who relieved
General Sigel. On May 27, equipped for rapid march-
ing, the regiment, with the army, advanced with little opposition until arriving in the vicinity of Pied-
mont, June 5, 1864. A battle here ensued, resulting
after severe and protracted fighting, in the total
rout of the enemy, and the capture of 1500 prison-

5

ers. Among the first mortally wounded on our side
was Adjutant Culver. While engaged with the regiment in one of the earliest charges made that day,
he was struck by a piece of shell and fell from his
horse.

Removed at once to the hospital, he died the following day, *June* 6, 1864. He had fought his last
fight, and received his death wound while joining in
the charge which brought victory to our arms.
What he had said he was willing to do, he was by
the providence · of God permitted to do in thus
cheerfully laying down his life for his country.

So the youth whom fond parents had watched as
he developed into all that was noble and pure, fell
bravely fighting for our liberties and our land. One
more name his death affords to the roll of heroes,
whose generous self-sacrifice sanctifies the cause. An
earnest Christian, a faithful clerk, a devoted patriot,
he has left behind the record of a noble life. Through
the casualty of battle he realized early and speedily
the lines of his favorite hymn—

    " Nearer, my God, to thee, nearer to thee,"

and the future opened to him a new life of nobler

aims and higher services. His firmly outlined integrity, united with his quiet enthusiasm had made him to be loved by many, and in this city he long will be remembered. In this epoch of grand events he acted a noble part, and sincerely and bravely performed his every duty.

Corporal HERBERT E. BECKWITH was born June 23, 1845. A youth of a thoughtful but reserved temperament, he was not by all understood or appreciated. The wayward impulses of a character not yet matured, were by some mistaken for the choices of a wilfull spirit. Yet all through his early years he exhibited some of the noblest traits possible to youth, blended with much that was strange and interesting. Pondering with more than a boy's usual seriousness the subject of religion, he frequently surprised them who knew him best by his earnest expression of the personal difficulties he met with in trying to heed its claims. Under the appearance of an eager, spirited life, lay concealed the thoughtfulness and lofty aspiration which really distinguished him. Many doubtless recall his slight form and pleasant face in the Sabbath School-room, where he was accustomed during the singing, to stand by the organ to work its bellows.

Early in the war he manifested a strong desire to enlist, but his youthful age and the wishes of his parents for a while deterred him. Many thought him too young to endure the hardships of a soldier's life, but the excitement and novelty of such a career had a fascination for him, and, boy as he was, he too felt the stirrings of that mighty passion which can make of the youngest, patriots and heroes. Not that he at this time thoroughly defined his motives, but it was more than idle curiosity that had made him wish to do what he instinctively felt was noble. To have part in the mighty conflict, was his strongest desire. He was a lad of noble impulses, and not unintelligently did he choose that his place should be among the brave defenders of his country.

After some debate as to the wisdom of such a course, he enlisted Oct. 1, 1861, in the Tenth Regiment, under Col. Russel. For nearly two years he shared the fortunes of that noble regiment. He passed safely through the battles of Roanoke Island, Newbern and Kinston. Through all this period till June, 1863, he acquitted himself well as a soldier.

His fragile form, and boyish countenance frequently excited the wonder how he should have come into the rough scenes and stern experiences of military life.

His Chaplain, Rev. H. C. Trumbull, testifies to his regular attendance at the regimental prayer-meetings, and on divine service. He appeared interested, and in many ways assisted the Chaplain in arranging for the different meetings to be held. Thus his influence and example were given to sustain the religious interests of the regiment. Undemonstrative in his feelings, it was his many kind acts and generally thoughtful manner, which indicated how much he valued the ministrations of his Chaplain.

At his father's request, he was honorably discharged, June, 1863. His soldierly conduct had gained him the esteem of both officers and men, and at the time of leaving he was to have been promoted to be Sergeant-Major. The remainder of the summer he spent at home, restlessly debating whether he ought not to enter the army again. He knew now what a soldier's fare was, and for one so young had already acquired considerable military experience. When proposing, therefore, a second time to

enter the service, it was with higher motives and a
better understanding of all it involved.   Talking
with his father about it, to the query: "suppose you
are wounded or killed?" he replied: "It is glorious to die for one's country." And I doubt not ,
that the training which had taught him to value our
Government and the institutions of freedom, had
wrought in him this willingness to do something for
their maintenance.

In November, 1863, he enlisted for the second time
in the Second Massachusetts Heavy Artillery. With
this regiment he left for Norfolk, Va., the following
month, and was stationed at Camp O'Rourke, near
the city.   On the 10th of January, 1864, he was
made Corporal, being detailed soon after as Orderly
to the Adjutant.   In February, the regiment was
ordered to Plymouth, N. C., where it performed gar·
rison duty, at Fort Wessels, one of the defences of
that place.   On the 20th of April Plymouth was at-
tacked by the enemy in force, and after a determined
resistance was captured.   Young Beckwith, with his
regiment, was among the prisoners taken.   They
were immediately marched off, and taken under
strong guard first to Tarboro, and thence to Wil-

mington, Charleston, and finally to Andersonville. Here five weary months were passed. Beckwith's journal gives his experience in that terrible prison-pen. It is substantially a history of suffering, cruelty and of every inhumanity possible to a desperate and unprincipled foe. "This is a miserable place," he writes in one place, "so little care is taken of it, especially of the sick, who die in large numbers." Exposure to the summer's scorching sun, and then to the night-dews, made its impress soon on the youthful soldier. It is painful to read of the struggle he and others had to make to live on the scanty and unwholesome rations dealt out there. On the 4th of July, he writes: "This most glorious day has passed almost in misery, in the most miserable place almost on earth." Sometimes he speaks of rations of rotten bacon, and again of the non-issue of the usual rations. The tale of suffering is affecting to read, and yet no word of complaint escapes him. Of his personal sufferings and patient hopeful spirit friends at home knew comparatively little, till companions of his escaped from that Pen of Death, and told what they witnessed. Their account of his hopeful courage and resolute endurance, was most

full and touching. Unable to digest the only food
furnished them, Beckwith was among the first to experience the pangs of unsatisfied hunger. His calm
relation in his diary of some terrible fact, such as
the failure of water, or the appearance of disease,
shows how the fearful schooling of these months had
familiarized him with the most excruciating suffering. Singularly reticent as to his own interior life,
he notes usually whatever he sees of interest. The
recurrence of the holy Sabbath appeared to make
him long most of all for his Christian home. "At
times," he says, "I fancy I hear the church bells in
Norwich."

Thus patiently the frail boy endured the weary
confinement which was gradually consuming his
strength, and destroying his health. Sept. 12th,
1864, came the welcome news of deliverance through
an exchange, and he left the prison, though with the
signs of a not far distant death. Taken to Charleston, he with the rest was transferred to one of our
transports, and brought North. December 24th, he
reached Camp Parole, Annapolis, Md., and on the
28th was removed to the hospital. Pale and weak,
with his lungs almost gone, after the exposures in-

cident to his prison-life, he went directly to his bed in the hospital, and died two days after, Dec. 30, 1864.

The Christian woman whose lot it was to nurse the wearied soldier-boy, writes after his death: "So feeble was he when he entered the hospital that he never spoke above a whisper. I questioned him as to his trust in his Saviour, asked him if he loved him, and whether he was willing to submit to His holy will, whether he should live or die. To all my questions he assented with a nod and a very sweet smile." So passed away the young veteran, not yet twenty years of age. By his services and his sufferings he honored his country. He died with a Christian's trust, and with a patriot's spirit—spared by a merciful providence till he reached friends and was under the old flag,—then the war-worn youth concluded his earthly campaigns, and like a tired child he sank to sleep, his day of duty ended.

Tidings of his arrival at Annapolis reached his parents too late for them to reach there before he died. His only wish was that "he might see his mother," and oftentimes the kind stroke of the woman's hand who watched him during his last days, would remind him of that other hand whose

6

touch he knew so well; and too weak to speak, he could indicate by a smile what he thought. His remains were brought home for interment, and all who looked upon the emaciated frame and saw the young face so traced with the lines of pain, received a new impression of the magnitude of some of our soldier's sufferings. Strange seemed the providence which had called the youngest and frailest of all who went from our School, to such an ordeal of hardship and suffering. Yet it was an ordeal which the delicate youth heroically passed through, dying a Christian's death, and without a murmur at the lot which had been his.

Captain JAMES R. NICKELS, was born in the town of Cherryfield, Maine, July 14, 1843. He was left an orphan at an early age, and having an aunt residing in this City, he came here in the year 1857, and attended school. In the winter of 1858, during a season of religious interest in the Central Baptist Church, he became personally interested, and requested the prayers of Christians in his behalf. These prayers he believed, as he afterwards publicly stated, God graciously answered to the salvation of his soul. Quite young at the time, his experience was not without many misgivings, but his subsequent career seemed to give every evidence that he had become an earnest Christian.

In the Spring of 1859, he entered the employ of R. M. Haven, and became a member of his family. At the outbreak of the war he enlisted in Captain (now Brig. Gen.) Harland's company, of the Third Connecticut Regiment, and passed creditably through the three months' campaign. His coolness at the Battle of Bull Run was noticed, where his company was one of the very few that suffered any casualties. Returning to his former business, he devoted his spare time to the study of military tactics. Such, however, was his patriotism, as well as his fitness for army service, that he could not remain contentedly at home.

He enlisted as a private once more in the Fourteenth Regiment, under command of Col. Dwight Morris. Offered the position of Lieutenant, he declined it in favor of one who had gotten more recruits than he, accepting the rank of First Sergeant. In less than a month, with little preparatory drill, or familiarity with actual service, the regiment was ordered to join the Potomac Army, and to take part in the bloody battle of Antietam. In December following it was in the fight at Fredericksburgh, where fourteen out of eighteen officers were killed or wounded. Nickels soon received the commission of Lieutenant, and in November, 1863, was promoted to the Captaincy of Company I. Up to this time his regiment had been almost constantly in active service. In the campaign of 1864, he passed through the terrible battles of the Wilderness unharmed, leading his regiment in a brilliant charge at Cold Harbor, for which he was complimented by the commanding General.

This hitherto uninterrupted career of success was terminated by a severe wound received in August, 1863, in the struggle for the possession of the Weldon Railroad. He was left on the battle-field, where he escaped being made a prisoner, because supposed to be dead. In the night, missed by his comrades he was sought out, and by the Adjutant and one other member of his company, was carried in the darkness a distance of eight miles. Thus, by the devotion of these friends was he brought within our lines. Taken to City Point, he was thence removed to Armory Square Hospital, Washington. Here, after a lingering illness, relieved at times by hopes of recovery, he died Feb. 20, 1865. During this long illness of nearly six months, he maintained a cheerful, patient spirit. His earnest wish was that he might regain his strength and return to the field, though he added: " I am not afraid to meet death." He looked upon all his sufferings as for the best, and sought bravely to suffer, if no longer he could *do* God's will. A few days before his death, says his aunt, when I told him his situation, and pointed him to Christ, he replied: " It is all right with me;" and soon he was loosed from his sufferings, and closed his young life calmly with a Christian's hope.

In his regiment, his gentlemanly conduct, his soldierly ability, his pure patriotism, had gained him a high reputation. As an officer he distinguished himself from the first, and by unquestioned merit, though among the youngest in the regiment, rose to be senior Captain. Modest in his bearing, his tact and courage were remarked by many. A brother officer of his regiment bears this noble testimony to the young soldier: "I never knew an order Capt. Nickels hesitated to obey, or the emergency he was

---

unequal to fill." In his hospital life he was watched
over by his aunt and brother, and during this weary
confinement, exhibited a cheerful, trustful spirit. Into twenty-one short years this orphan boy crowded
a life-time of noble deeds. He left behind the name
and record of a Christian patriot. His short career
was a brilliant and useful one; and none think of him
now without grateful acknowledgment of all that
he was permitted to do. Of his appearance in the
Sabbath School, his teacher writes: "Young Nickels
was a very pleasant scholar, quiet and thoughtful, an
attentive listener, very seldom absent from his seat,
and unusually observant of the proprieties of the day
and place. This recollection of him is distinct—that
he was not one of those whose attention was so easily
diverted as to task all the teacher's ingenuity in order to keep his mind to the business of the hour.
He was never forward to express his thoughts,
but when he did so, it was because he had thoughts
to express. This was especially noticeable on one
of those first exciting Sabbaths after the war commenced, when he told of his fixed determination to
take a personal share in the struggle. It was hardly

expected by me, considering his seeming frailty of
body, and his usual undemonstrative manner."

Faithful in the store, he was esteemed by his employers, while as a soldier of his country he gained
his brightest laurels in its service. Rescued from the
mediocrity which envelopes so many names, this orphan shall be made known to fame; for holy impul-
pulses of patriotism and heroic suffering have exalted his memory and his achievements. Such heroes
gave to our struggle its sacredness; such sacrifices
endear every privilege we through them obtain.
God seemed to accept these young defenders of a
country he has so marvellously befriended,—for in
all these instances, none were left to die uncheered
by the anticipations of Heaven.

Such were the brave youth who went from our
School and Church to battle and die for the country.
Such was the patriotism which we may gratefully
believe was helped in its development by the religious inspiration gained here. Regretfully as we
may sometimes think of these young men so early
sacrificed, yet the cause they served, the results their
sacrifice helped to secure, compensate in a measure for
our bereavement. Such a record as they have left

of piety blended with patriotism, honors us. Their
history is a beautiful testimony to the spirit which
characterized our Church and School during those
years of peril and sorrow to the nation. Surely, to
cherish the memory and example of these young
heroes should be our grateful duty, and will not be
unprofitable.

We have not mentioned CHARLES E. BREED, who
dying after discharge from the service, thus fails to
come within the scope of this Memorial. Nor have
we spoken of others who were spared by a protect-
ing providence to return to us; though the survey
of all that they attempted and accomplished is
fraught with most stirring interest, exciting our
reverent affection and just pride.

Not many Schools of Christ can show a nobler
record of unselfish devotion, high-hearted patriotism, and splendid achievement. Especially would
we render our tribute to the brave boys who fell
fighting in our defence; and though their graves
are not all with us their memories linger, sacredly
embalmed in all our hearts. How grand is our history when seen through the medium of such lives
as these. How precious the new Freedom won by

their patriotic valor. Reviewing at a glance the trophies of these crucial years, it is plain that the death of these young men was not a vain sacrifice. Their courage has attained for them a renown which will never grow old; their achievements have given new glory to the land, new value to the Government. The benign institutions which are the dear purchase of their blood, perpetuate their fame, and press home upon us our solemn obligations. Henceforth all who deny that our liberty can be combined with law, justice and the advancement of happiness, we point to these names. Those who doubt whether our Government can produce exaltation of soul and loyalty to what is just, we refer to the achievements of these heroes, who went forth in their young strength to do battle for sacred but imperilled rights. Beautiful in the Christian hope each cherished, heroic in their patriotic services, happy in their early but triumphant deaths,—what a record they have left behind.

It is well and fitting, therefore, that we enshrine in Memorial phrase, names that will ever live as symbols of nobleness, as signs of endearment. Beautiful the life and true, that leaves holy deeds to witness that it has been.

7

And so long as our own now prosperous nationality exists, with the dust of heroes in its soil, with its examples of the prowess of the past, and its prophetic visions of the future, so long will these young patriots be remembered.

Though these rare hearts have stilled forever their fevered beating, and faces yet traced with tears of bereavement show they are mourned, still will we thank God they were permitted to toil, to suffer, and to die. Nobly they labored, and with holy gratitude we enter into their labors. Wiser laws, humaner institutions, liberties enlarged and faith exalted—these are the crimsoned trophies their blood, with that of others, secured us. These shall proclaim in a language more expressive than human lips can utter, in forms more significant than sculptured marble can exhibit, the worth and memory of the young men who sowed in weakness the harvest we raise in power.

Let the voice of our brothers' blood cry to us from the ground, kindling in every heart a chastened but resolute enthusiasm to extend through the land the blessings of our regenerated liberties. Let a fraternal spirit awaken a new emulation in advancing all the great branches of industry, in promoting the free institutions of Government, and procuring establishments for education, charity and moral improvement, in teaching a better religious faith and a greater consecration to what is just and pure.

"How sleep the brave who sink to rest
With all their country's wishes blest!
When Spring with dewy fingers cold,
Returns to deck their hallowed mold,
She there shall dress a sweeter sod
Than fancy's feet have ever trod.
There Honor comes, a pilgrim gray,
To bless the turf that wraps their clay—
And Freedom shall a while repair,
To dwell a weeping hermit there."

APPENDIX.

CHARLES EDWARD BREED was born in Norwich, Sept. 19, 1845. Without any thing of note to mark his early days, he had quietly yet faithfully met the duties of school and business life. At the beginning of the war he manifested an earnest desire to enlist in his country's service, but feeble health and the wishes of friends deterred him. Still retaining his interest in the cause he from the first desired personally to aid, he finally decided, with the consent of his parents to enter the navy, in April 1864. Not able even then to endure a soldier's hardships, he hoped to be of some service to the Government on one of its vessels, while also anticipating that the sea-air might benefit his health. With a generous feeling that what he could, he ought to do, he took his place on the ship, and by faithful unpretentious duty rendered his share in the crushing out of rebellion. The exposures and labors of his position, however, proved too much for his strength, and reluctantly, though after persistent trial, he was obliged to seek discharge from duty. He came home in February of '65, with the symptoms of fatal disease. Lingering till the following April, he grew weaker and weaker, when, like the expiring taper, his life quietly went out. So gradually and yet certainly he came to his end, that from almost the first he and his family gave up all hopes of recovery. Young in years and delicate in appearance, his was a short career; but we can not forget even the brief service of those whose patriotic purposes exceeded their powers of execution. Like many other wearied and weak ones, the war hastened the consummation of the life that but for it, might have been prolonged. The fire of a noble patriotism consumed some, as exhausting toil broke down others. But better the purpose, though it find but partial realization, than length of days unsanctified by any lofty aim. God often removes those who have early planned for useful living, while he waits long for others to make even the faint beginnings of true devotion. Heaven will thus behold the full fruitage of many lives from which earth anticipated benefits.

The following are the names of all those who entered the army or navy, and had been previously connected with the Congregation or Sabbath School. The dates when they enlisted and when they were mustered out of service are given, together with the rank they held at the time the latter occurred.

A large proportion began their military career as privates, or non-commissioned officers, and earned their promotion by their ability and courage in the field. All will regard it as a noble record of patriotic achievement. It is moreover quite remarkable that out of so large a number sent forth to battle for their country, so few were killed; for all the regiments with which these young men were connected met severe service, and many were the hardships personally encountered. The experience of some who have returned attest how much was suffered by our soldiers; for they were in perils by the sword, by prison, by weariness, by cold, on sea and land. Several lived through the horrors of the "Andersonville Pen," and others endured long confinement in Libby Prison.

The fruits of their own labors God has kindly permitted them to behold and enjoy. They survive a conflict, the magnitude of which time will disclose, and the full significance of which other ages will see. They have borne an honorable part in a contest which has done more than any other history records, to establish human liberty and popular government. A share in the blessings their invincible valor procured is their happy lot, and the

country for which they have fought will be endeared to them as
to no others.

The consciousness of having done their duty must in every
case increase their enjoyment of present and future civic privi-
leges. Their brave deeds will not soon be forgotten, while all entering into their labors will cease not in grateful remembrances
of their toils and sufferings. The cause they shone in, is itself
immortal, and their names forever blended with it, can never pass
away:

SAMUEL T. C. MERWIN, Capt.   Apr. 22, 1861, June 27, 1865.

WM. G. ELY, Col.   "   "   Sept. 18, 1864.

DAVID YOUNG, Lt. Col.   May 7, 1861, Aug. 7, 1861.

FRANK S. CHESTER, Capt.   "   "   "   "

JOSEPH H. JEWETT, Adj't.   "   "   Dec. 12, 1865.

FRANCIS McKEAG, 2d Lt.   "   "   June 27, 1865.

JAMES McKEE, Serg't.   "   "   "   "

HENRY F. COWLES, 1st Lt.   "   "   May 15, 1865.

JAMES R. NICKELS, Capt.   May 11, 1861, Died Feb. 20, '65.

JAMES TORRANCE, Serg't.   "   "   kill'd May 24, '63.

PARRIS R. NICKERSON, Corp.   "   "   Aug. 12, 1861.

H. W. BIRGE, Brevet Maj. Gen. May 23, 1861, Oct. 1865.

JOHN A. BECKWITH,   Sept. 21, 1861, Sept. 20, 1864.

HERBERT E. BECKWITH, Corp.   Oct. 1, 1861, Died Dec. '30, 64.

CHARLES M. COIT, Capt.   Oct. 5, 1861, May 30, 1865.

JAMES E. FULLER, Capt.   Apr. 24, 1861, res'd July 6, 1865.

EDWIN F. HINCKLEY,   Oct. 26, 1861, Nov. 3, 1862.

SILAS W. SAWYER, Capt.   Oct. 30, 1861, res'd. Feb. 16,'64.

Chas. Farnsworth, Lt.Col.	Nov. 26, 1861, res'd. May 17,'64.
Alfred P. Rockwell, Col.	Jan. 21, 1862, Feb. 9, 1865.
Alfred Mitchell, Capt.	Feb. 18, 1862, res'd. Mar. 11,'64.
William P. Miner, 1st Lt.	" " July 16, 1864.
Bela P. Learned, Maj.	Mar. 12, 1862, Sept. 25, 1865.
Frank S. Bond, Major.	March, 1862, Nov. 10, 1864.
Alvan Bond Fuller,	May, 1862, May, 1865.
Henry P. Goddard, Capt.	June 11, 1862, res'd. Apr. 26,'64.
Leonard Simons,	Aug. 23, 1862, June 10, 1865.
Isaac W. Hakes, Jr., Capt.	July 12, 1862, res'd. Dec. 26,'62.
Wm. C. Hillard, Hosp'l. St'd.	July 14, 1862, Nov. 26, 1865.
David Torrance, Lt. Col.	July 17. 1862, Nov. 24, 1865.
Anthony Adams,	" " June 27, 1865. '
Joseph P. Rockwell, Capt.	July 26, 1862, " "
E. Benjamin Culver, Adjt.	" " killed June 6, '64.
George W. Loomis, Serg't.	" " June 27, 1865.
Christopher A. Brand, 1st Lt.	" " res'd. Feb. 23,'63.
D. W. Hakes, Capt. and Com.	Aug. 4, 1862, June 17, 1865.
Henry K. Sparks,	Aug. 5, 1862, June 27, 1865.
George Coggswell, Serg't.	Aug. 6, 1862, " "
James N. Clark,	Aug. 25, 1862, Aug. 17, 1863.
Stephen B. Meech, Adj't.	Aug. 30, 1862, " "
Subert M. Porter,	" " " "
C. B. Webster, A. A. Surg.	Dec. 24, 1862, Sept. 11, 1865.
Alfred M. Goddard, 1st Lt.	July 24, 1863, died May 9, 1864.

N

GEORGE W. HUNTINGTON,

    U. S. N. Paymaster,   Oct. 30, 1863, Nov. 21, 1865.

AMOS D. ALLEN, U. S. N. Pm'r. Nov. 1, 1863, Sept. 5, 1865.

C. E. BREED, U. S. N. 3d Eng'r. April 14, 1864, died Apr. 17, '65.

JOSEPH ABBE,   Mar. 22, 1864. May 30, 1865.

www.ingramcontent.com/pod-product-compliance
Lightning Source LLC
Chambersburg PA
CBHW031747090426
42739CB00008B/915